The Quilt for a Cure
SAMPLER

Designed by Marti Michell

Better Homes and Gardens® *American Patchwork & Quilting*® has featured an annual sampler quilt since its first year of publication. A block from each issue is selected to be part of the year-end Sampler. Because *American Patchwork & Quilting* is a bi-monthly magazine, each sampler quilt had been developed with only 6 blocks until 1997. That year, each issue contained a quilt I had designed using two blocks. At the end of the year, twelve blocks were used in the Sampler Quilt.

When it came time to select a fabric group for the Sampler, I was very attracted to a pretty blue and yellow floral at the Northcott–Monarch booth at Quilt Market. When I took Heidi Kaisand, the editor of *American Patchwork & Quilting*, to see the fabric, we discovered that it had been designed by Bonnie Benn Stratton under the QUILT FOR A CURE™ banner. Portions of the proceeds from the fabric sales go toward the Breast Cancer Research Foundation. This made it perfect—a beautiful fabric and a good cause! It also explains why the 1997 *American Patchwork & Quilting* Sampler that I designed was frequently called "the Quilt for a Cure Sampler."

So now it is official! The October 1999 issue of *American Patchwork and Quilting* announced this booklet and previewed the remake of the 1997 sampler in Stratton's Fine China Blue Quilt for a Cure fabric collection, as shown on the cover of this booklet.

We Hope You Will...

Feel free to use this pattern to create raffle or opportunity quilts to raise funds for Breast Cancer research, awareness or patient therapy. You may forward funds directly to the Breast Cancer Research Foundation, but please make reference to the "Quilt for a Cure" campaign. You may also feel free to donate any funds raised to local agencies or causes. Please drop us a note; we would love to know of your results.

Our Thank You

Thank you for purchasing this book. Michell Marketing has joined the Quilt for a Cure campaign and will contribute $1 to the Breast Cancer Research Foundation for every Quilt for a Cure Sampler Book sold. Stratton and Northcott–Monarch both donate portions of the proceeds from Quilt for a Cure fabrics to the Breast Cancer Research Foundation, see page 2 for more information. Thank you for helping!

Marti Michell

This booklet is dedicated to all women and men who face the challenge of breast cancer and to the fight for a cure. We also dedicate it to our family members:

Alta Riddle Glenn *1907–1994*
Marti Michell's mother and a breast cancer survivor.

Gladys Turley Michell *1908–1955*
Richard Michell's mother, a victim of cancer during the infancy of cancer research.

Sarah Whittinghill Samuelson Trask *1913–*
Ann Davis Nunemacher's aunt and a forty year breast cancer survivor.

Mary Gladys Dinkel *1910–1969*
Richard Dinkel's mother and a victim of breast cancer.

The fact is this: Breast cancer is the leading cause of death among women between the ages of 35 and 54. It strikes one woman in eight. Every eleven minutes a woman dies from breast cancer. This year 180,000 women will be diagnosed. No one is immune. The older we grow, the more we are at risk. Everyone is aware of this devastating disease—if you or someone in your family has not been personally affected, you know someone who has. The keys to combating these alarming odds are individual awareness, responsibility and increased funds dedicated to research.

October is "Breast Cancer Awareness Month." Across the country businesses participate by displaying the pink ribbon emblem, by providing educational literature and by sponsoring public service announcements encouraging annual mammograms. But Quilt for a Cure can be a year-round project.

The Quilt for a Cure campaign was initiated by Bonnie Benn Stratton, whose mother is a breast cancer survivor. When Bonnie began to design fabrics for Northcott–Monarch, she realized a way that she could participate in the fight against breast cancer. Both Bonnie and Northcott–Monarch donate a portion of the purchase price of every single yard in all of the Stratton Collections to The Breast Cancer Research Foundation in behalf of Quilt for a Cure. Michell Marketing is proud to be joining in this effort with a $1 donation for each of these booklets sold.

Quilt for a Cure has been publicized by all of the major quilting magazines. T-shirts and tote bags with the Quilt for a Cure logo are available through Merryvale, Ltd., 11416 Vale Road, Oakton, VA 22124 (703-264-8959). The eye-catching items were designed to publicize the campaign as well as raise awareness and funds for the Foundation.

The Breast Cancer Research Foundation

Founded by Evelyn Lauder, The Breast Cancer Research Foundation (BCRF) is a not-for-profit organization dedicated to finding a cure for breast cancer through research. Since the BCRF is largely underwritten, over eight-five percent of all funds raised goes directly to grants for clinical research to the following major medical centers across the United States:

American Health Foundation, Inc. – NY

Cancer and Leukemia Group B – IL

*Children's Hospital/
Harvard Medical School – MA*

Cold Spring Harbor Laboratory – NY

Georgetown University Medical Center – DC

The Johns Hopkins Oncology Center – MD

Mayo Clinic – MN

Mayo Clinic – FL

*Memorial Sloan-Kettering
Cancer Center – NY*

Sarah Lawrence College – NY

Swedish Medical Center Tumor Institute – WA

University of California – CA

University of Illinois at Urbana – IL

Indiana University – IN

*University of North Carolina/
Lineberger Center – NC*

*University of Pennsylvania
Cancer Center – PA*

*University of Texas/J. D. Anderson
Cancer Center – TX*

University of Washington – WA

The Foundation welcomes and depends upon contributions from all those concerned with women's health. It is our hope that by working together, we will conquer this disease in our lifetime.

THE BREAST CANCER
RESEARCH FOUNDATION
767 Fifth Avenue, 46th Floor
New York, NY 10153
Phone: 212-572-4249
FAX: 212-572-5766
bcrf@estee.com
www.bcrfcure.org

In Praise of Sampler Quilts

It is said that variety is the spice of life. That must be one of the reasons I love Sampler quilts. They are fun to make and easy to enjoy! When I started quilting, I was very attracted to Sampler quilts, the name given to quilts with a different design in every block. After the rotary cutter was developed in 1979, I became fascinated with strip techniques, and making sampler quilts didn't fit into that style. Then, in 1995, when we started manufacturing acrylic templates for rotary cutting, I realized how easy it would be to make sampler blocks when I had permanent templates. It has been great to have sampler quilts back in my quilting repertoire.

Sampler quilts are wonderful because:

- Each block gives you the opportunity to experiment with different fabric combinations.

- Each block gives you a chance to use different sewing techniques and to develop new skills.

- You can't get bored making dozens of the same block. Samplers are great for people with short attention spans! Of course, I insist that isn't why I love sampler quilts.

- Historically, it is believed, sampler quilts served as a "reference library" of quilt blocks for pioneer quiltmakers. They can serve the same purpose for you.

- The Quilt for a Cure Sampler is quite organized, but once you are comfortable making sampler quilts, you will probably find they can be a great home for some of the orphan blocks you may have.

Selecting Fabrics for a Sampler Quilt

By combining my experience in making sampler quilts with years of appreciating both antique and newly-made samplers, I have made several observations about selecting fabrics for samplers.

Select a Theme Fabric

A theme fabric or focus fabric is very important to visually hold the quilt together. Whether it is multi-colored or monochromatic, this fabric generally establishes the color scheme for the quilt. My favorite type of theme fabric is a medium to large scale multi-color fabric. It is frequently the final border, but should be used quite liberally in the quilt interior, too. Small multi-color prints don't work well for theme fabrics as the colors tend to blur when you aren't very close to the quilt.

In this particular quilt, the theme fabric will probably be used in the six alternate blocks.

Select at least Seven More Fabrics

It seems to me that the most successful sampler quilts are made with a good variety of fabrics to match the variety of blocks. Seven fabrics, in addition to the theme fabric, would be the minimum number I would use, and I really prefer more fabrics. (See three examples on the inside front cover.) A good way to expand the number of fabrics in a quilt is to select three or four similar fabrics for every fabric in the key. Then select from the group when that fabric is indicated.

If you are using unpieced blocks, as shown in this quilt, make sure the fabric you have selected for the sashing contrasts adequately with those blocks. The fabric that creates the star points in the sashing can be strong or subtle; it is your choice.

When you have selected at least eight fabrics for your quilt, my observation is that working several of them into every block helps to make the blocks in the quilt look united. Nearly every block could be made with only two or three fabrics. That is, there would be enough contrast to see the distinct patchwork shapes.

However, by increasing the number of fabrics in each block, the quilt is unified because each block carries the entire color scheme of the quilt.

Select for Variety

Your quilt will be more interesting made with fabrics in a variety of colors, scales and textures. Think small to large designs, light to dark colors, and geometric to floral looks. Be sure to include a variety of printed textures for a more interesting quilt.

Select an Accent Fabric

An accent fabric of ½ yard or less may be the most important fabric you choose. Judiciously used, this accent fabric adds sparkle and creates the feeling of motion as your eye is attracted to different parts of the quilt. The accent fabric can be difficult to select if you are picking fabric in the store and looking at equal size bolts of every fabric. Try to look at your fabric selections proportionately.

New Block Designs

In addition to the 12 original blocks used in the first Sampler, this booklet includes 10 new blocks. These were selected so you could have 16 blocks for the King-size version of the Sampler, to balance the use of the template sets, and to give you more choices.

Both of the Quilt for a Cure fabric collections used for the quilts shown included beautiful choices for alternate non-pieced blocks. However, in another fabric combination, you might want to make 18 patchwork blocks. If you want to substitute patchwork blocks for the alternate empty blocks in the King size layout, you'll need 25 blocks. Select one block that you would like for all four corners. The 21 additional blocks will complete the quilt.

In other fabrics, the quilt looks so different that we think you may want to use this layout again and with the addition of new blocks you will have more choices.

The original quilt had blocks using Sets A, B, C, D & E of the **From Marti Michell** Perfect Patchwork Templates. If you own any of those five **From Marti Michell** Template Sets, each of them has instructions for 6 free 12-inch blocks on the package inserts.

Not all blocks look good when set on point. Since the 12-inch blocks in this quilt are set on point you need to think about that before substituting other blocks. Looking at the 30 blocks on the insert sheets for Sets A–E, I felt there were only three or four that wouldn't be attractive on point.

How to Make and Use a Design Wall

A design wall is a wonderful tool that can easily be set up in part of your studio. It can be as elaborate or as simple as your space and budget allow. The ultimate design wall would be to cover an entire wall of your studio with felt or bulletin board material, so you can position fabrics and stand back to study the effect. The simplest is a piece of batting temporarily taped to a wall or wrapped abound a large bulletin board or piece of foam core from the art supply store.

If you aren't using the Fine China Blue collection and the fabric keys as shown, I highly recommend using a design wall while making Samplers. In this quilt, the first thing to do is decide which fabric you think will be sashing, sashing blocks, alternate squares and setting triangles. Cut a few pieces of each and position them on your design wall leaving space for patchwork blocks.

Now you can audition fabrics for the block in relationship to the things around the block. As you cut pieces for the first block, put them in place on the design wall. It is better to make your fabric decisions based on what is best for the quilt, not specifically for the block.

To help you decide on fabrics and position I sometimes rough cut fabrics and shapes, but with a sampler quilt like this, it is nearly as easy to cut the actual pieces and position them. Stand back and look. We seldom see a quilt at only an arms length, but that is the view we get when sewing or quilting. It is very important to look at a block from across the room. Then if you like the arrangement, you are ready to sew. If you don't like it, simply

cut different fabrics, one may be all you need to replace, or you may need to start from scratch. Either way, there is a good chance that before you finish the quilt the replaced cut pieces will fit into another block.

Is there enough contrast between the outside edge of the block and the sashing? In the Fine China Blue cover quilt, the background fabric that most frequently is on the block's edge is the lightest fabric in the quilt and the sashing is a medium dark fabric.

Let me share one tip I have learned (the hard way, of course). Sometimes an absolutely beautiful block just doesn't look right in the quilt. Usually if a block doesn't fit the quilt it is because the background, generally those pieces of the block that touch the sashing, is a different value than the background fabrics in most of the other blocks.

Stand back and look again. Did you use a good variety of fabrics? Remember, a good variety of fabrics in each block unifies the quilt.

Even when you are satisfied with the first block, you may want to cut a second or third block and put them on the design wall and look at them all together for balance before you start sewing.

Cutting Strips First

No matter which shapes you are cutting, it is most common to first cut a strip that is the same width as one dimension of the desired piece, then use the template to create the desired shape. Most frequently people use a 6″ x 24″ (15.2 x 61 cm) acrylic ruler to measure and cut strips. I prefer to cut my strips on the lengthwise grain.

When the strip widths for Set L pieces came out to sixteenths and thirty-seconds of an inch, it caused an obvious realization—Use the template to measure the width of the strips. Necessity truly is the mother of invention! The template is the exact size, and it is a measuring tool. It just isn't what we are used to calling a ruler. The technique is shown below, illustrated with templates from Set A.

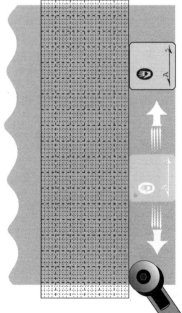

Use squares for measuring strip widths when possible. Straighten the edge of the fabric, and align the template with the raw edge. Place your ruler against the template to mark the cutting edge.

Slide the template along the raw edge to be sure the ruler is correctly aligned, then remove the template and cut the strip.

- Place the template on the strip to cut the shape. Don't forget to slip a small cutting mat under the strip as you cut the shapes and nip the corners.

- The desired grainline affects the orientation of a triangle template on the strip and, thus, the width of the strip.

Understanding Grainline Arrows

The acrylic Perfect Patchwork Templates and the patterns in this booklet that duplicate their size all carry a recommended grainline cutting arrow. The arrow should lay on the straight lengthwise grain whenever possible. The arrows were selected for the most common use of the template. However, the same template may have different edges on straight grain at different times. This can even happen in the same block!

If there is no grainline arrow in our individual block illustrations, it means to cut as recommended on the template or pattern. If there is an arrow in the illustration, it overrides the arrow on the template. Design issues in fabric, such as directional prints, always override recommended grainline guidelines.

Cutting Pairs

When pieces of the same shape are going to be sewn together, it is often advantageous to cut the pieces together. Layer the fabrics right sides together, cut the strips and then the desired shapes. The pieces will already be properly positioned for sewing, a great time-saver. Lift them carefully and move to the machine.

Half-square triangles can almost always be cut together and they are used so frequently that if time and accuracy are important to you, it is important to get in the habit of cutting the pieces together. The same is true of most squares for four patch sections.

Cutting 2 + 2 Triangles

In several block patterns, you will find two right triangles cut from the same fabric and sewn together, back to back. Often that seam can be eliminated. In appropriate places this has been done and is marked in the template designator boxes. In several of the blocks, the largest right triangle in the set must be flipped to create the larger unseamed triangle. You will see the piece designated as 2 + 2. The good news is that the uniquely engineered corners make some clever tricks possible.

1. Cut strips the same width as for the regular triangle. Position the triangle and make the first diagonal cut.

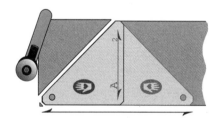

2. Flip or rotate the template and align it with the straight edges and the corner angles and make the second cut. The seam allowances are automatically removed and the cut 2 + 2

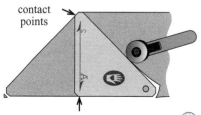

contact points

triangle is exactly the same size as two #2 triangles cut individually and sewn together.

Cutting Fake Diamonds

Two right triangles can be sewn together to look like a diamond, but they really make a parallelogram, or a "fake diamond." Often the seam between the triangles can be eliminated.

In fact, right triangles can be used to make parallelograms in two different orientations.

In the first orientation, the legs are on the straight grain of the fabric. You would cut the strip the width of the leg.

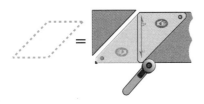

In the second orientation, the hypotenuse is on the straight grain and you would cut the strip the narrower width.

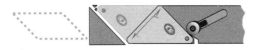

Any Perfect Patchwork Template right triangle can be used to create a parallelogram.

Cutting parallelograms is similar to cutting the 2 + 2 triangles. Make the first diagonal cut.

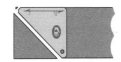

Then flip the template and align it with the straight edges of the

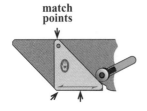

match points

6

strip so the corner angles fit in place with the first cut you made. Make the second diagonal cut.

Parallelograms are asymmetrical. In most cases you need mirror image pieces. For that you will want to cut pairs, right sides of the fabric together. If you need matching parallelograms, all pointing the same way, multiple layers of fabric must face the same direction (right side up or right side down).

Use this trick carefully. See the block called Four Corners Squared on page 20. The parallelogram was cut in one color only and all of the construction is straight-line sewing. If parallelograms had been cut in both colors, it would have resulted in set-in corners that are much more time consuming.

See the block called Four Corners Squared on page 20.

Basic Sewing Methods

There are several classic construction techniques that are repeated in several blocks. If you are new to quilting, some of the terms and methods may not be familiar to you. We have chosen to describe and illustrate them once here.

Using 1/4" Seam Allowances: a Must

With strip-technique quilts, consistency in your seam allowance is enough. With blocks like these where you are using varying shapes and angles, that is not true. Now, the key to sewing perfect points and blocks that are all exactly the same size is sewing an exact 1/4-inch seam allowance.

Quarter-inch seam allowances are included in both the printed pattern pieces and the templates. That means 1/4" seams are a must! Test yours by cutting three 2-inch by 5-inch strips and sewing them together lengthwise. The sewn unit should measure 5 inches square. More importantly, the finished size of the center strip should be a perfect 1 1/2 inches wide. If you don't get these measurements, make an adjustment and repeat the exercise.

Making Four Patch Units

Place the two fabrics right sides together in sets of four before cutting strips; the order is dark, light, light, dark. Then cut the squares and nip the corners. Chain piece, picking up two pieces at a time so they don't shift out of alignment. The fabric that is on top alternates automatically. Press seam allowances toward the dark square. Cut the chain apart in pairs. Place the pairs right sides together and sew into a four-patch.

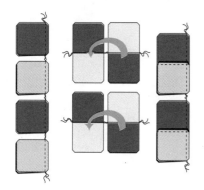

Chain Piecing Flying Geese

1. Chain piece first small triangle to the large triangle. Press toward the smaller triangle, regardless of color.

2. Add second small triangle. Press toward small triangle again.

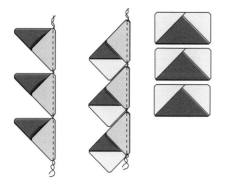

Making the Square within a Square

Many of the blocks in this quilt feature this construction technique. You will especially enjoy the engineered corners in this step. Always sew two triangles on opposite sides of the square. Press seam allowances toward the triangles and then sew the triangles to the other side to create the new square.

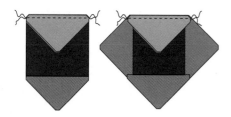

Making the Eight-pointed Star Blocks

Several blocks include 45-degree diamonds that make the classic eight-pointed star. Follow these basic instructions for those blocks.

1. Join diamonds into pairs, sewing dot-to-dot.

Sewing Tip: Sewing Dot-to-Dot

Dot-to-dot piecing ensures sharp, accurate points on diamonds and other angular shapes. The holes in the templates are cut precisely to fit a sharp pencil or other marker. If using the patterns, carefully mark the placement of the dots on your fabric pieces. Mark the seam intersections with the dots, then stitch perfect ¼-inch seams between the dots. This method leaves the seam allowances free so that they can be pressed out of the way as you sew.

If you are used to taking a backstitch at both ends of each seam, try replacing backstitches with a very short stitch, at each end of a dot-to-dot seam.

2. Set a square into each pair using two separate dot-to-dot seams.

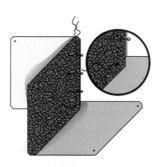

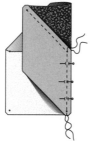

3. Sew pairs of diamond pairs together to make half-stars and set a triangle into each half.

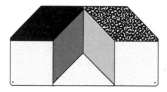

4. Sew the two halves together using two seams, lifting the seam allowances so that they are not sewn in place. Set a triangle into the remaining sides.

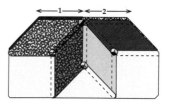

5. Press the block carefully, fanning the seam allowances at the block center in a circular manner to reduce the bulk at the center.

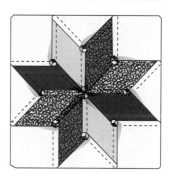

Making Flaps

The throw and the individual block wall hanging are both accented with flaps. Flaps are like piping without the cord. They can be added between the quilt interior and first border, between borders, or between the border and the binding.

To make flaps, cut fabric strips between ⅞- and 1¼-inch wide on the lengthwise grain and as long as the quilt, piecing diagonally if necessary. Fold in half lengthwise with wrong sides together. Align raw edges and stitch a scant ¼-inch from the edge. Sew a flap on one side, then the opposite side, then the remaining sides. Then proceed.

What Size is a Quilt?

The desired finished size of a quilt is very personal. The guidelines I use were developed by adding a 9-inch pillow tuck at one narrow end and a 13-inch drop to the other three sides of the most common mattress sizes. There have to be compromises. All quilt sizes aren't easily divisible by all block sizes, etc. There will be some size loss during quilting; the amount varies with the type of batting and density of quilting. If you didn't wash your fabric before cutting and piecing, there will be shrinkage when you wash the quilt.

About the Borders on These Pages

The border measurements given in these charts are mathematically correct for the blunt finish borders illustrated. For information on mitered borders, see page 24.

Always measure your quilt before cutting and adjust borders, if necessary.

Measurements listed are *cut* measurements. See page 26 for approximate yardage requirements for these four sizes.

Throw Size Sampler —55½″ x 77″

See throw on inside front cover.

Mattress size:	not applicable
Interior (without borders):	42¼″ x 63½″ (107.3 x 161 cm)
Blocks: 6	12½″ (31.75 cm) square
Alternate blocks: 2	12½″ (31.75 cm) square
Sashing: 24 strips	3½″ x 12½″ (9.9 x 31.75 cm)
Setting squares: 7	Template 1, Set A
Half-squares: 10	Template 2, Set A
First Border	
Sides: 2 strips	1¾″ x 64″ (4.4 x 162.5 cm)
Top/Bottom: 2 strips	1¾″ x 45¼″ (4.4 x 114.9 cm)
Second Border	
Sides: 2 strips	6″ x 66½″ (15.2 x 168.9 cm)
Top/Bottom: 2 strips	6″ x 56″ (15.2 x 142 cm)

Twin Size Sampler—61″ x 98″

Mattress size:	39″ x 75″
Interior (without borders):	42¼″ x 84½″ (107.3 x 214.6 cm)
Blocks: 8 or 11	12½″ (31.75 cm) square
Alternate blocks: 0 or 3	12½″ (31.75 cm) square
Sashing: 24 strips	3½″ x 12½″
Setting squares: 10	Template 1, Set A
Half-squares: 16	Template 2, Set A
First Border	
Sides: 2 strips	2¼″ x 85″ (5.7 x 215.9 cm)
Top/Bottom: 2 strips	2¼″ x 46¼″ (5.7 x 117.5 cm)
Second Border	
Sides: 2 strips	8″ x 88½″ (20.3 x 224.8 cm)
Top: 1 strip	3½″ x 62¾″ (8.9 x 159.4 cm)
Bottom: 1 strip	8″ x 62¾″ (20.3 x 159.4 cm)

Full/Queen Size Sampler

This quilt size is a compromise between queen and double size quilts. It is a very luxurious size for a double, but the drop might not be as long as you like on a queen, especially if you have the newer 9-inch mattress. The drop, however, is easily adjusted by border width as you can see by the different sizes of the two cover quilts.

Finished quilt size:
With borders shown here and on front cover	82½″ x 104″ (209.5 x 264 cm)
With borders shown on back cover	87¼″ x 109 ¾″ (221.6 x 278.8 cm)

Mattress size:
Full	54″ x 75″
Queen	60″ x 80″

Interior (without borders):	63½″ x 84½″ (161.3 x 214.6 cm)
Blocks: 12	12½″ (31.75 cm) square
Alternate blocks: 6	12½″ (31.75 cm) square
Sashing: 48 strips	3½″ x 12½″
Setting squares: 17	Template 1, Set A
Half-squares: 14	Template 2, Set A

First Border
Sides: 2 strips	2¼″ x 85″ (5.7 x 215.9 cm)
Top/Bottom: 2 strips	2¼″ x 67½″ (5.7 x 171.5 cm)

Second Border
Sides: 2 strips	8″ x 89″ (20.3 x 226 cm)
Top/Bottom: 2 strips	8″ x 82½″ (20.3 x 209.5 cm)

King Size Sampler—106″ square

Mattress size:	78″ x 80″
Interior (without borders):	84½″ (214.6 cm) square
Blocks: 16	12½″ (31.75 cm) square
Alternate blocks: 9	12½″ (31.75 cm) square
Sashing: 64 strips	3½″ x 12½″
Setting Squares: 34	Template 1, Set A
Half-squares: 16	Template 2, Set A

First Border:
Sides	2½″ x 85″ (5.7 x 215.9 cm)
Top/Bottom	2½″ x 89½″ (5.7 x 227.3 cm)

Second Border:
Sides	9″ x 89½″ (22.9 x 227.3 cm)
Top/Bottom	9″ x 106″ (22.9 x 269.2 cm)

Measurements listed are *cut* measurements. See page 26 for approximate yardage requirements for these four sizes.

This illustration is of the quilt shown on the cover. From left to right, the blocks are Carolina Lily, Sweet Sixteen, Postage Stamp Basket, Northern Lights, Cheerio, Pinwheel Variable Star, Dutchman's Pinwheel, Churn Dash, 54-40 or Fight, Sister's Choice, Rambler, Corn 'n' Beans. Select any 12 of the 22 blocks shown in this book, or use any of your favorite block designs, and arrange as desired.

Fabric Key for Quilt for a Cure Sampler
For your convenience, there is also a fabric key with each block.

Fabric, by Position in Quilt	Key in Book	Snippet of My Fabric
Theme fabric – alternate squares, final border and blocks		Paste fabric in these boxes.
Setting and Corner Triangles		
Sashing and use in blocks		
Sashing Triangles and use in blocks		
Sashing Squares		
Narrow Border and blocks		
Light background in blocks		
Use in blocks		
Use in blocks		
Use in blocks		

11

54–40 or Fight

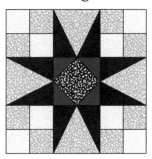

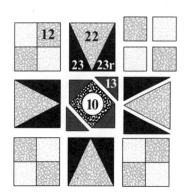

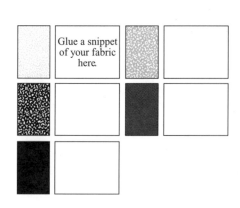

Sets B and D, pieces 10, 12, 13, 22 and 23.

Cutting

With piece 10, cut 1

With piece 12, cut 8 and 8

With piece 13, cut 4

With piece 22, cut 4

With piece 23, and the fabric layered right sides together, cut 4 pairs of triangles.

Assembly

Assemble into 9 sub-units.

Chain piece 8 pairs of squares into 4

Add a piece 23 to each 22 and press open,

then add 23r.

Using the square within a square method on page 7, add triangles to opposite sides of piece #10. Press and add the two other #13 triangles.

Arrange the 9 sub-units and stitch into rows. Sew rows together into the 54-40 or Fight block.

Carolina Lily

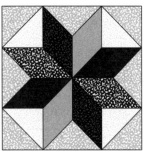

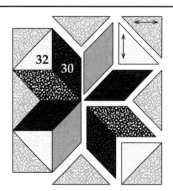

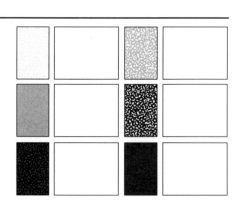

Set E, pieces 30 and 32.

Cutting

With piece 30, cut 2 of each

With piece 32, cut 8,

4 with 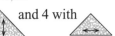 and 4 with

With piece 32, cut 4 with

Assembly

Sew together the half-square triangles whose legs were cut on the straight grain to make corner squares.

Follow basic instructions for making the Eight-pointed Star, page 7, to complete the Carolina Lily block.

Cheerio

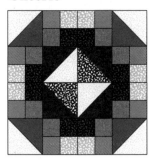

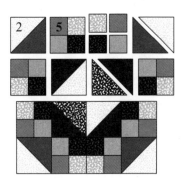

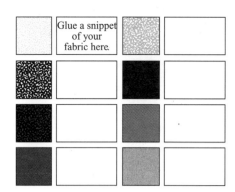

Set A, pieces 2 and 5.

Cutting

With piece 2 and fabrics right sides together, cut 4 ◺ and 4 ◥

cut 2 ◣ and 2 ◸

cut 2 ◣ and 2 ◹

With piece 5 and right sides together,

cut 8 ▨ and 8 ▦

cut 8 ▢ and 8 ■

Assembly

Following the fabric key of the block diagram, chain piece appropriate triangles into 8 squares.

Chain piece small squares into 16 pairs then 8 four patch units.

Lay out 16 sub-units into rows, as shown above, and assemble into the Cheerio block.

Churn Dash

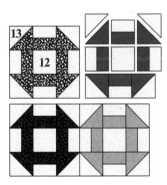

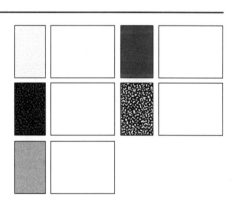

Set B, pieces 12 and 13.

Cutting

With piece 12, cut 4 ▢

From each of 4 fabrics cut strips 1½″ x 10½″.

From background fabric cut four strips 1½″ x 10 ½″.

With piece 13, cut 4 ◺ each of fabrics ▨▦ ■▦

cut 16 ◺ of background fabric.

Assembly

Chain piece pairs of colored triangles and background triangles.

Chain piece all 4 colored strips to background strips. Press, then cut 4 squares (#12) from each color combination of strips.

Make 4 small Churn Dash units, putting the same fabric in each sub-unit:

Join the four small Churn Dash units into the Churn Dash block.

13

Corn 'n' Beans

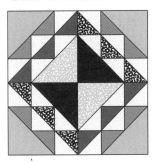

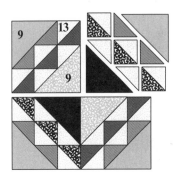

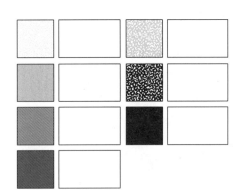

Set B, pieces 9 and 13.

Cutting

With piece 9, cut 2

cut 2

cut 4

With piece 13, cut 8

cut 20

cut 6

cut 6

Assembly

Chain piece 6 and 6 triangles with background triangles to make squares:

Add background triangles as shown to assemble rows.

Join rows to make 2 of each:

Add large triangles to each side of these units. Assemble the four quarter-blocks into Corn 'n' Beans, as shown.

Dutchman's Pinwheel

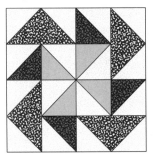

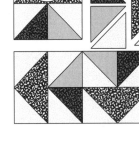

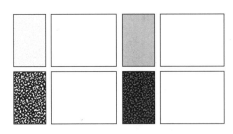

Set A, piece 2

Cutting

With piece 2, cut 4
See page 5.

Cut 16

Cut 4

Cut 4

Assembly

Assemble into sub-units:

4

Use flying geese method shown on page 7.

Chain piece remaining triangles into squares.

4

4

Join sub-units into quarter-blocks.

Join the four quarter-blocks into the Dutchman's Pinwheel, as shown.

Northern Lights

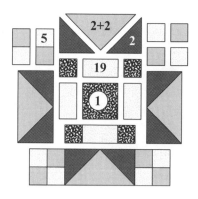

Sets A and C, pieces 1, 2, 5, and 19.

Cutting

With piece 2, cut 8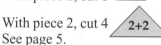

With piece 2, cut 4
See page 5.

With piece 5, cut 4

With piece 5 and rights sides together, cut 8 ☐ and 8 ▢

With piece 1, cut 1

With piece 19, cut 4 ☐

Assembly

Chain piece 8 pairs. ☐☐

Join into squares. ▦

Using the Flying Geese method on page 7, add 8 ◣ to 4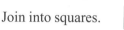

Make center unit by adding 2 rectangles to square 1 on opposing sides.

Press toward center square.

Add 1 square to each end of the remaining #19 pieces. Press toward the squares.

Add to top and bottom of the center unit.

Position and assemble into 3 rows. The middle row will be twice as wide as Rows 1 and 3.

Assemble rows into Northern Lights block.

Pinwheel Variable Star

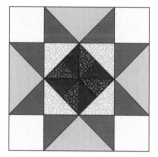

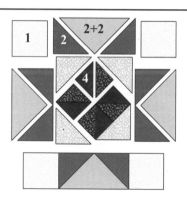

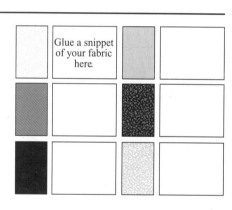

Set A, pieces 1, 2 and 4.

Cutting

With piece 1, cut 4 ☐

With piece 2, cut 8 ◣

cut 4 ◺

With piece 2, cut 4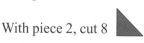
See page 5.

With piece 4 and right sides together, cut 4 ◣ and 4 ◣

Assembly

Chain piece small triangles into squares and join squares to make the pinwheel.

Using the square within a square method, add triangles to pinwheel square.

Make 4 Flying Geese sub-units; see page 7.

Make three rows. The middle row will be twice as wide as Rows 1 and 3.

Assemble the rows to make the Pinwheel Variable Star block.

Postage Stamp Basket

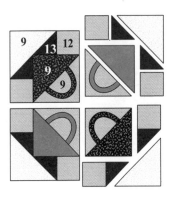

Glue a snippet of your fabric here.

Set B, pieces 9,12 and 13 plus handle pattern or bias strips

Cutting

With piece 9, cut 4 ◿   cut 4 ◿

           cut 2 ◿   cut 2 ◿

With piece 12, cut 8 ◻

With piece 13, cut 8 ◤

Cut handles to match basket triangles.

Use pattern on page 29 or cut bias strips 1½" x 7½" long and steam press into shape.

Assembly

Applique (or fuse) handles on appropriate triangle of background fabric. Add basket triangle to each handle triangle.

Sew 4 each

Add to basket sections, then add the final triangle.

Press. Each small block should be 6½". Join small blocks into Postage Stamp Basket.

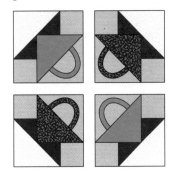

Rambler

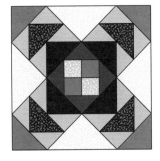

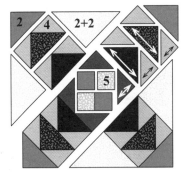

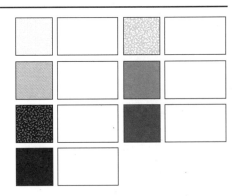

Set A, pieces 2, 4 and 5.

Cutting

With piece 2, cut 4 ◺ See page 5.

With piece 2 and legs on straight grain, cut 4 ◿

With piece 2 and the hypotenuse on straight grain, cut 4 ◿

and cut 4 ◿

With piece 4 and the legs on the straight grain, cut 16 ◿

            cut 4

With square 5, cut 2 each

Assembly

Make four patch of small squares.

Using square within a square method, page 7, add triangles on two opposite sides of center square.

Make 8 Flying Geese units and assemble with remaining 2 triangles into 4

Add 2 of these units to opposing sides of the center square unit.

Add 2+2 triangles to both sides of the remaining Flying Geese units and complete the Rambler block.

 16

Sister's Choice

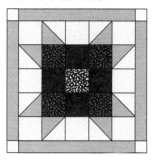

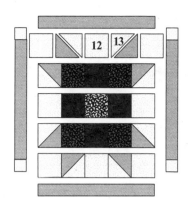

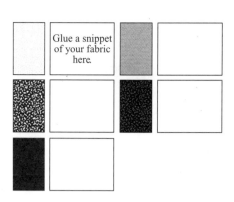

Set B, pieces 12 and 13.

Cutting

Cut 4 1½″ corner squares. □

Cut 4 1½″ x 10½″ framing strips.

With piece 12, cut 4 ▓

cut 4 ■

cut 8 □

cut 1 ▨

With piece 13 and fabrics right sides together, cut 8 ◸ and 8 ◿

Assembly

Chain piece the triangles into squares. Arrange all of the squares into the five rows shown.

Take advantage of directional pressing. Press seam allowances in the opposite directions in alternate rows so the seams will butt together as the rows are sewn.

Add framing strips to top and bottom. Add corner squares to remaining framing strips and add to remaining sides to complete the Sister's Choice block.

Sweet Sixteen

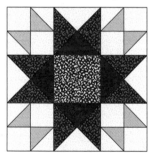

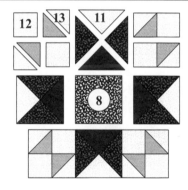

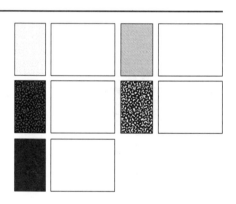

Set B, pieces 8, 11, 12 and 13.

Cutting

With piece 8, cut 1

With piece 11, cut 4 ▽

cut 8 ▼

cut 4 ▼

With piece 12, cut 8 □

With piece 13 and fabrics right sides together, cut 8 ◺ and 8 ◿

Assembly

Sew into 9 equal-size squares. Press and use piece 8 to true-up if necessary.

For this unit

assemble 4

and 4

All triangle pairs must be sewn in the same orientation for the pieced squares to match. Press seams as shown, and complete final seam.

Assemble into rows.

Assemble rows into Sweet Sixteen block.

17

Bluegrass Needles

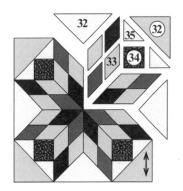

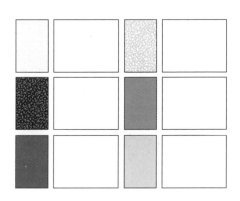

Set E, pieces 32, 33, 34 and 35, optional 30.

Cutting

With piece 32, cut 4

And with legs on the straight grain, cut 4

With piece 33, cut strips and then cut 16

cut 8

cut 8

With piece 34, cut 4 ▦

With piece 35, cut 8 ◺

Assembly

Make 8 large diamonds by combining 8 pairs

8 pairs

Press toward darker fabric and combine pairs to make a larger diamond. Use pattern 30 to confirm true diamond shape of pieced diamonds.

To assemble corner units add a piece 35 to piece 34,

then add another piece 35.

Press toward square and join to a piece 32 to complete corner sub-units.

Follow basic Eight-pointed Star instructions, page 7, to assemble the Bluegrass Needles block.

Buds of Paradise

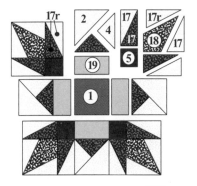

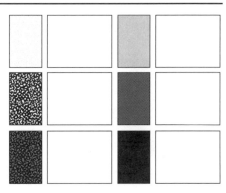

Sets A and C, pieces 1, 2, 4, 5, 17, 18 and 19

Cutting

With piece 1, cut 1 ▦

With piece 2, cut 4 ◺

With piece 4, cut 4 ◣

cut 4 ◺

With piece 5, cut 4 ■

With piece 18, cut 4

With piece 17 and right sides

together, cut 8 pairs of

and 4 pairs of

With piece 19, cut 4

Assembly

Add a 17 to each 18

Press and add 17r to the other side.

Join contrasting pairs of 17 and 17r as illustrated. Only the long edge aligns, not the corners!

Use square 5 to complete 4 units for the corners.

Sew 4 pairs of piece #4 triangles. ◣

Add piece 2 to each pair.

Add piece 19 to the proper side.

Arrange sub-units in rows and assemble into three rows, then finally into the block.

Cabbagetown

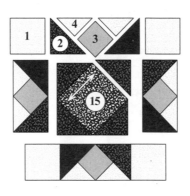

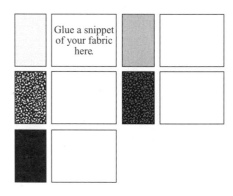

Sets A and C, pieces 1, 2, 3, 4 and 15

Cutting

With piece 1, cut 4

With piece 2, cut 8

cut 4

With piece 3, cut 4

With piece 4, cut 8

With piece 15, cut 1

Assembly

Add 4 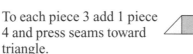 to center square using the square within a square method on page 7.

To each piece 3 add 1 piece 4 and press seams toward triangle.

Then add another piece #4 to the pair.

Using flying geese method, page 7, to add and to pieced triangle.

Join sub-units into 3 rows. The middle row will be wider than rows 1 and 3.

Join rows to form the Cabbagetown block.

Diamond in the Rough

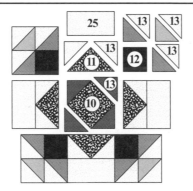

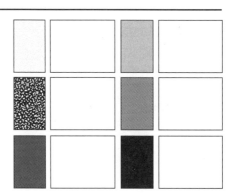

Sets B and D, pieces 10, 11, 12, 13 and 25

Cutting

With piece 10, cut 1

With piece 11, cut 4

With piece 12, cut 4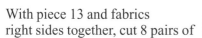

With piece 13 and fabrics right sides together, cut 8 pairs of

cut 4 pairs of

Then cut 8  and 4

With piece 25, cut 4

Assembly

Think of the Diamond in the Rough as having nine sub-sections.

Chain piece the 12 pairs of half-square triangles of piece #13:   4   8

Combine these 12 pieced squares with the #12 square to make 4

Combine piece #10 with 4 pieces #13 using the square within a square

method on page 7 to make the center unit.

Using the Flying Geese method on page 7, add 8 #13 triangles to the 4 #11 triangles.

Add a piece #25 to the top of the Flying Geese just assembled.

Arrange sub-sections into 3 rows, and assemble rows into the Diamond in the Rough block.

19

Double Starlight

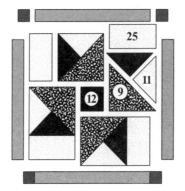

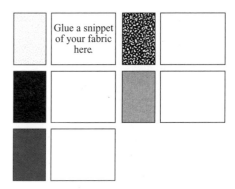

Sets B and D, pieces 9, 11, 12 and 25

Cutting

Cut four 1½″ corner squares.

Cut four 1½″ x 10½″ framing strips.

With piece 9, cut 4

With piece 11, cut 4

cut 4

With piece 12, cut 1

With piece 25, cut 4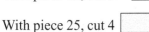

Assembly

Join the triangle 11 pairs.

Add the triangle 9 pieces.

Add the rectangle to the side with the dark small triangle.

Use a partial seam technique for final assembly. Place the center square on one of the four units. Stitch halfway and press open, as shown.

Continuing clockwise, join each section. After the fourth section, go back and complete the first seam.

Add the frame as described in Sister's Choice, page 17.

Four Corners Squared

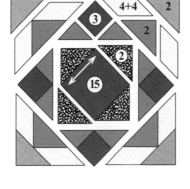

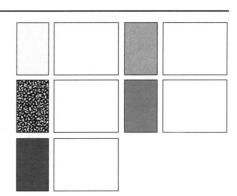

Sets A and C, pieces 2, 3, 4 and 15

Cutting

With piece 2, cut 4

cut 4

cut 4

With piece 3, cut 4

With piece 4, cut 8

Cut 4 pairs 4 + 4; see page 7.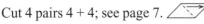

With piece 15, cut 1

Assembly

Use the square within a square method, page 7, to add four triangles to the square.

To assemble the next round of corners, chain piece 4

Press open and add 4 more triangles to make 4

Add to opposite sides of center unit.

Add a 4 + 4 parallelogram to each side of a #2 triangle to make 4

Add final triangle to these units and then add completed corners to center section.

Grandmother's Favorite Star

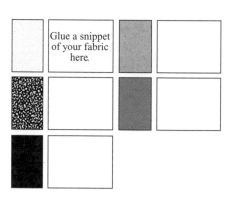

Glue a snippet of your fabric here.

Sets A and E, pieces 2, 4, 33, 34 and 35

Cutting

With piece 2, cut 12

cut 4

With piece 4, and legs on the straight grain, cut 4

and cut 4

With piece 4, and hypotenuse on straight grain, cut 8

With piece 33, cut 4

cut 4

With piece 34, cut 4

With piece 35, cut 4

Assembly

Join 4 ◢ and 4 ◥

Join 4 ◣ and 4 ◤

with legs on straight grain.

Combine ◢◣

and add a triangle. Make 4

Add triangle #2 in the Flying Geese style to each sub-unit to make 4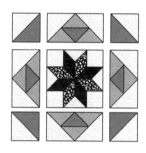

Make 6″ star using basic Eight-pointed Star instructions, page 7.

Assemble sub-units into rows and the rows into Grandmother's Favorite Star.

Ice Cream Social

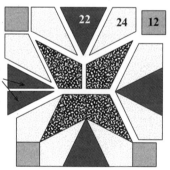

Option: Use 23 & 23r to make perfect quarter blocks.

Sets B and D, pieces 12, 24, 22 or 23

Cutting

With piece 12, cut 4

With piece 22, cut 4

Or substitute piece 23 and cut 8, fabrics right sides facing, so there are 4 #23 and 4 #23 reversed.)

With piece 24, cut 4

cut 8

Assembly

This is a very unusual arrangement of pieces, that is what I like about it; but frankly, this use of pieces #24 and #22 weren't even imagined when the template corners were engineered.

The pieces do not align at the corners the way we love them to, but the edges do fit perfectly for sewing. Add a #24 to each side of #22 to make 4

Join 4 pieces #24 to make center unit.

Also, there are no holes ¼-inch from the edge for marking.

Review dot-to-dot sewing, page 7. You must stop ¼-inch from the tip of piece 24 (as marked with circles) on your own when using that version.

Substituting the 8 small 23 triangles means you can make edge to edge seams everywhere except at the corner where square #12 is set in.

21

Lillian's Flower Basket

Sets B and E, pieces 9, 12, 13, 30, 32, 34 and 35; optional, 33.

Cutting

Cut two background strips as wide as piece 12 and 9″ long.

With piece 9,

cut 3   cut 1   cut 1

With piece 13, cut 2

With piece 32, cut 2

With piece 34, cut 3 ■ and 3 □

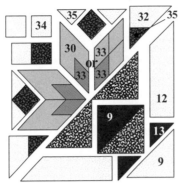

With piece 35, cut 4 △ and cut 2 ▲

For the four large diamonds, choose applique or piecing. **Either** use piece 30 and cut 4 ◇ and with piece 33, cut 4 ◇ and applique #33 onto #30,

Or using instructions in Bluegrass Needles, page 18, make 4 large diamonds from 12 #33 ◇ and 4 #33 ◇

Assembly

To make basket, join ◩

Add a triangle 9 to one side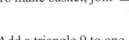

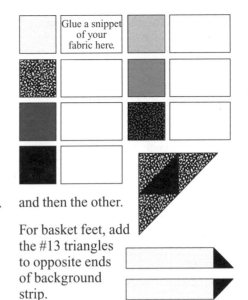

and then the other.

For basket feet, add the #13 triangles to opposite ends of background strip.

Sew strips to basket. Trim ends of strips even with basket and add final triangle.

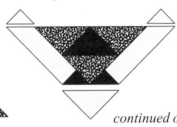

continued on page 30

Weathervane Plus

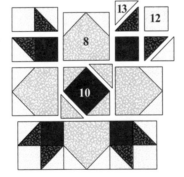

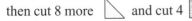

Set B, pieces 8, 10, 12 and 13

Cutting

With piece 8, cut 4 ▦

With piece 10, cut 1 ■

With piece 12, cut 4 ■

and cut 4 □

With piece 13 and right sides of fabric together, cut 8 pairs

then cut 8 more and cut 4

Assembly

Chain piece 8 pairs of triangles

Join with squares to make 4

Using square within a square technique on page 7, make center unit.

On each of the large squares, place one of the #13 triangles, face down. Special corners will line

up perfectly with the sides of the square. Stitch ¼″ from edge of triangle.

Press a triangle onto the corner of the square and confirm that the edges match. Cut away excess fabric from square.

Repeat on other corner.

Assemble sub-units into three rows. Sew the rows together to complete the Weathervane Plus block.

The Quilt for a Cure Sampler

FINISHED SIZE:

Individual Blocks: 12 inches square (30.5 cm)

Quilt: 82½ x 104 inches (209.5 cm x 264 cm) with borders shown on front cover

87¼ x 109¾ inches (221.6 x 278.8 cm) with borders on back cover

MATERIALS REQUIRED:

4 to 5⅝ yards theme fabric. Used in 6 center squares, last border and blocks.

    4 yards with no special cutting, *or*

    5⅝ yards Fine China Blue, as shown on cover

1¼ yard setting and corner triangles

2 yards sashing and blocks

1¾ yards sashing triangles and blocks

⅜ yard sashing squares

1 yard narrow border and blocks

Fabric used only in blocks:

1½ yds. light background

¾ yards light medium; in the cover quilt, baby blue

½ yard medium

½ yard Dark; in the cover quilt, a large floral

⅞ yard for French fold binding (For cover quilt, it can be cut from the 5⅝ yards of theme fabric.)

6¼ yards of backing fabric

Batting, at least 4″ (10cm) bigger in both directions than the quilt top.

Instructions are for the queen/double quilt. See pages 8 and 9 for layouts and basic information for other sizes. See page 26 for approximate yardage requirements for all sizes. Substitute the appropriate number of blocks, sashing strips, etc., for whichever size quilt you have chosen. Please read all directions before beginning.

It is exciting to be able to present in one booklet the 1997 *American Patchwork and Quilting* Sampler, affectionately known as The Quilt for a Cure Sampler and now officially carrying that name. The blocks are set diagonally, with sashing that features stars at each intersection. All of the fabrics on the front cover are from the Northcott–Monarch Fine China Blue Collection by Bonnie Benn Stratton. All of the fabrics on the back cover are from the Northcott–Monarch Plantation Collection by Bonnie Benn Stratton. In both collections there were fabrics that made wonderful alternate blocks in the Sampler quilt.

Select and Make the Desired Number of Blocks

The Fine China Blue cover quilt was made using the same 12 patchwork block designs used in the original sampler. This booklet includes all of them and 10 new blocks. Choose your favorite and make the number needed for your quilt. If you have chosen the Fine China Blue fabric, you can just follow the key for fabric position that is included with each block and the quilt. If not, see page 3 regarding fabric selection. Also, there were several more fabrics used in the quilt on the back cover and you may want to look at that picture and make variations in your patchwork blocks based on that.

The blocks should all be 12½ inches (31.75 cm). Check sizes and make any alterations necessary now. If blocks are all a little larger or smaller, you can adjust the length of the sashing pieces to fit. However, if only one or two blocks are considerably off-size by ½–¾-inch, think "pillows," and make new blocks.

Naturally, we used the **From Marti Michell** Perfect Patchwork acrylic templates for rotary cutting to make the quilt. The corners are engineered to make pieces match perfectly and the seam allowances are included. Ask for the templates at the same store where you bought this booklet or you can make templates from the patterns on pages 28-30. See "Basic Cutting Tips and Tricks" on page 5 if you have not used the templates before.

Cutting the Components

You probably cut some alternate blocks and sashing strips if you were auditioning fabrics for blocks. After confirming that they are 12½ inches square, cut the rest of the alternate blocks and pieced sashing. But first:

1. Reserve at least 32 inches by 108 inches of the border fabric, the minimum amount needed for unpieced borders to be cut on the lengthwise grain. Then cut:

- 6–12½″ squares for alternate blocks, centering the design in each. Because these squares are cut diagonally, there will be large triangular scraps. Use them for pieces in the blocks.

To speed cutting on the sashing pieces, multiple layers of strips are cut first. Then use templates or patterns to cut the desired shapes from layered fabric strips.

2. From the sashing fabric, cut a total of:

- 48–3½" by 12½" sashing strips. Align Triangle 16 with each end and sides of the strips, and use it as a guide to cut away the ends of each strip. (If you are using a paper pattern as a guide, be careful that you do not trim the pattern.)

3. Fold the triangle fabric right sides together, then cut:

- 6–3⅝" x 27" strips (a total of 12 strips). Stack several pairs of strips, with each pair right sides together, and cut 192 of Triangle 17.

4. From the fabric chosen for the sashing squares, cut:

- 17 of Square 1 (3½" square).

- 14 of Triangle 2. Typically, these would be cut with the hypotenuse on the straight grain. Strips would be 2⅝" wide. However, with the check fabric in this quilt, the legs are on the straight grain, placing the hypotenuse is on the bias; handle carefully!

Piece and Add the Sashing Strips

1. Sew two of Triangle 17 into place at each end of each sashing strip.

2. Press triangles away from sashing and repeat with remaining triangles.

3. After determining the proper orientation for all of the sampler and alternate blocks, chain piece a sashing strip to the lower side of each of the 18 blocks.

4. Join a Square 1 to one end of 17 sashing strips.

5. Chain piece sashing strip-and-square combinations to the left side of 14 of the blocks.

6. Join the remaining Triangle 2 pieces to the end(s) of the last 13 sashing strips to complete the layout on the next page.

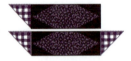

Assemble the Quilt Interior

Because the Sampler Quilt features a diagonal set, setting and corner triangles are required to fill in the outer edges of the quilt interior.

1. From the fabric chosen for the setting blocks, cut:

- 3–18¼" squares. Cut each

square twice diagonally to yield 12 setting triangles. Ten are required.

- 2–9⅞" squares. Cut each square once diagonally to yield four corner triangles.

2. Lay out the blocks, remaining sashing, and setting and corner triangles in diagonal rows.

3. Add the sashing to the blocks and triangles as required to complete each row. Join the rows. Add the corner triangles to complete the quilt interior. The quilt interior should measure 64 inches by 85 inches including ¼-inch seam allowances.

Adding Borders

Before attaching the border, you must first think about how you like it to look. Do you prefer to sleep with the border on top of a bed and would never pillow tuck, you may want to reduce the size of the top and save quilting time.

Before adding the border, you must decide whether to use a blunt- or mitered-corner border.

[Handwritten note on pink paper, overlaid:]
Points yellow
setting
corners — plaid
solid blocks &
border —
yellow/pm
sashing —
corner triangles
et, pts

[Handwritten note left margin:]
3er 16 strip

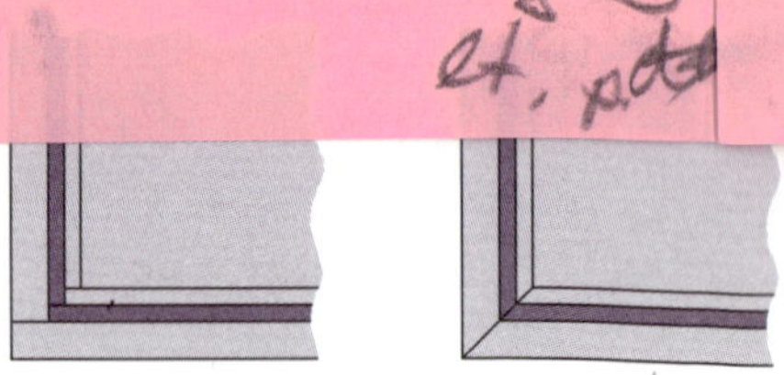

Blunt   **Mitered**

The cover quilts have mitered corners because the linear design of the fabric will look great with a mitered border. Most quilts I make have blunt corners.

There are several reasons I don't do many miters. Mitered corners take more time, more fabric, more skill and lots more luck than blunt corners. An even better reason is that, when the same non-directional fabric is being used in the entire border, the resulting corners look the cut first. Then use templates or patterns to cut the desired shapes from layered fabric strips.

2. From the sashing fabric, cut a total of:

- 48–3½″ by 12½″ sashing strips. Align Triangle 16 with each end and sides of the strips, and use it as a guide to cut away the ends of each strip. (If you are using a paper pattern as a guide, be careful that you do not trim the pattern.)

3. Fold the triangle fabric right sides together, then cut:

- 6–3⅝″ x 27″ strips (a total of 12 strips). Stack several pairs of strips, with each pair right sides together, and cut 192 of Triangle 17.

4. From the fabric chosen for the sashing squares, cut:

- 17 of Square 1 (3½″ square).

- 14 of Triangle 2. Typically, these would be cut with the hypotenuse on the straight grain. Strips would be 2⅝″ wide. However, with the check fabric in this quilt, the legs are on the straight grain, placing the hypotenuse is on the bias; handle carefully!

Piece and Add the Sashing Strips

1. Sew two of Triangle 17 into place at each end of each sashing strip.

2. Press triangles away from sashing and repeat with remaining triangles.

3. After determining the proper orientation for all of the sampler and alternate blocks, chain piece a sashing strip to the lower side of each of the 18 blocks.

4. Join a Square 1 to one end of 17 sashing strips.

5. Chain piece sashing strip-and-square combinations to the left side of 14 of the blocks.

6. Join the remaining Triangle 2 pieces to the end(s) of the last 13 sashing strips to complete the layout on the next page.

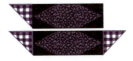

Assemble the Quilt Interior

Because the Sampler Quilt features a diagonal set, setting and corner triangles are required to fill in the outer edges of the quilt interior.

1. From the fabric chosen for the setting blocks, cut:

- 3–18¼″ squares. Cut each square twice diagonally to yield 12 setting triangles. Ten are required.

- 2–9⅞″ squares. Cut each square once diagonally to yield four corner triangles.

2. Lay out the blocks, remaining sashing, and setting and corner triangles in diagonal rows, (see diagram next page).

3. Add the sashing to the blocks and triangles as required to complete each row. Join the rows and add the corner triangles to complete the quilt interior.

The quilt interior should measure 64 inches by 85 inches including ¼-inch seam allowances.

Before Cutting Borders

Before deciding on final borders, you will want to think about how you like to dress a bed. If you prefer to stack pretty pillows on top of a quilt and would never use a pillow tuck, you may want to reduce the size of the top border and save quilting time.

Before cutting fabric for borders, you must decide whether to add blunt finish or mitered borders.

 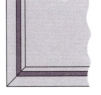

Blunt   **Mitered**

The cover quilts have mitered corners because the linear design of the fabric will look great with a mitered border. Most quilts I make have blunt corners.

There are several reasons I don't do many miters. Mitered corners take more time, more fabric, more skill and lots more luck than blunt corners. An even better reason is that, when the same non-directional fabric is being used in the entire border, the resulting corners look the

The Quilt for a Cure Sampler

FINISHED SIZE:

Individual Blocks: 12 inches square (30.5 cm)

Quilt: 82½ x 104 inches (209.5 cm x 264 cm) with
     borders shown on front cover

     87¼ x 109¾ inches (221.6 x 278.8 cm) with
     borders on back cover

MATERIALS REQUIRED:

4 to 5⅝ yards theme fabric. Used in 6 center
squares, last border and blocks.

    4 yards with no special cutting, *or*

    5⅝ yards Fine China Blue, as shown on cover

1¼ yard setting and corner triangles

2 yards sashing and blocks

1¾ yards sashing triangles and blocks

⅜ yard sashing squares

1 yard narrow border and blocks

Fabric used only in blocks:

1½ yds. light background

¾ yards light medium; in the cover quilt, baby blue

½ yard medium

½ yard Dark; in the cover quilt, a large floral

⅞ yard for French fold binding (For cover quilt, it
can be cut from the 5⅝ yards of theme fabric.)

6¼ yards of backing fabric

Batting, at least 4″ (10cm) bigger in both directions
than the quilt top.

*Instructions are for the queen/double quilt. See
pages 8 and 9 for layouts and basic information for
other sizes. See page 26 for approximate yardage
requirements for all sizes. Substitute the appropriate
number of blocks, sashing strips, etc., for whichever
size quilt you have chosen. Please read all
directions before beginning.*

It is exciting to be able to present in one booklet the 1997 *American Patchwork and Quilting* Sampler, affectionately known as The Quilt for a Cure Sampler and now officially carrying that name. The blocks are set diagonally, with sashing that features stars at each intersection. All of the fabrics on the front cover are from the Northcott–Monarch Fine China Blue Collection by Bonnie Benn Stratton. All of the fabrics on the back cover are from the Northcott–Monarch Plantation Collection by Bonnie Benn Stratton. In both collections there were fabrics that made wonderful alternate blocks in the Sampler quilt.

Select and Make the Desired Number of Blocks

The Fine China Blue cover quilt was made using the same 12 patchwork block designs used in the original sampler. This booklet includes all of them and 10 new blocks. Choose your favorite and make the number needed for your quilt. If you have chosen the Fine China Blue fabric, you can just follow the key for fabric position that is included with each block and the quilt. If not, see page 3 regarding fabric selection. Also, there were several more fabrics used in the quilt on the back cover and you may want to look at that picture and make variations in your patchwork blocks based on that.

The blocks should all be 12½ inches (31.75 cm). Check sizes and make any alterations necessary now. If blocks are all a little larger or smaller, you can adjust the length of the sashing pieces to fit. However, if only one or two blocks are considerably off-size by ½–¾-inch, think "pillows," and make new blocks.

Naturally, we used the **From Marti Michell** Perfect Patchwork acrylic templates for rotary cutting to make the quilt. The corners are engineered to make pieces match perfectly and the seam allowances are included. Ask for the templates at the same store where you bought this booklet or you can make templates from the patterns on pages 28-30. See "Basic Cutting Tips and Tricks" on page 5 if you have not used the templates before.

Cutting the Components

You probably cut some alternate blocks and sashing strips if you were auditioning fabrics for blocks. After confirming that they are 12½ inches square, cut the rest of the alternate blocks and pieced sashing. But first:

1. Reserve at least 32 inches by 108 inches of the border fabric, the minimum amount needed for unpieced borders to be cut on the lengthwise grain. Then cut:

   • 6–12½″ squares for alternate blocks, centering the design in each. Because these squares are cut diagonally, there will be large triangular scraps. Use them for pieces in the blocks.

To speed cutting on the sashing pieces, multiple layers of strips are

pattern will meet at the corners. A second option is to center the space between two large designs.

Cut the fabric for the first border:
- 2–2 ¼-inch by 69-inch strips
- 2–2 ¼-inch by 90-inch strips

Cut fabric for the outside border:
- 2–8-inch by 87½-inch strips
- 2–8-inch by 106½-inch strips

All four borders must be positioned perfectly and sewn to all sides of the quilt, stopping ¼-inch from the end of the quilt at every corner. Press the seam allowances toward the quilt interior.

To stitch a traditional miter, fold the quilt top at a 45-degree angle with the borders perfectly aligned on top of each other. Continue the fold line with the stitching.

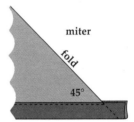

After sewing the first border in place, use a rotary cutter to trim excess fabric beyond the seam allowance.

Continue with additional borders or sew borders together first and miter both at the same time.

Using a Mock Miter

When I do miter the corners, they are usually mock mitered. The instructions are the same up to the miter. Then you work from the front of the quilt with one border extended flat and the other folded and pressed to make the perfect 45-degree angle. Pin in place and carefully stitch by hand with a hidden stitch. Trim away excess fabric.

same whether they are blunt-seamed or mitered.

Adding Mitered Borders

These instructions are for the Fine China Blue quilt (see cover) with two borders with mitered corners. The Plantation quilt (see back cover) was finished with three borders with mitered corners; this quilt is larger than the one shown on the front cover. You should do what is right for the quilt you have made and appropriate for the size quilt you need.

Borders that will be mitered have to be cut longer than blunt finish borders. To the length or width of the quilt, you must add two times the width of the border and two seam allowances to determine the length of each border.

Once again, please look at both cover quilts. If you are using a border fabric with large motifs, they will be more attractive if carefully positioned and symmetrical. The easiest way to plan this kind of border is to center one motif on all four sides of the quilt. Check how the

Using Blunt Corners

To add blunt corner borders, determine the desired width of the quilt border, add seam allowances and cut strips to match the length of the quilt plus seam allowances.

Pin in place, matching the center points, quarter points and eighth points of both the quilt and the border strip. Add side borders first. Then repeat for the top and bottom borders. Repeat for as many borders as you have chosen to use.

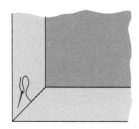

Complete the Quilt

Layer the quilt top, batting and backing. Quilt as desired. The cover quilt was machine quilted with invisible thread in the ditch on all of the pieced blocks. Stitching criss-crosses the sashing between star points to create diamonds. There is stipple quilting in the alternate blocks and a continuous line fan shape and diagram (see pattern on page 27) in the setting triangles.

French Fold Binding

Bind using your favorite method. I prefer a French-fold binding cut on the straight grain. French-fold bindings are cut four times as wide as the desired finished width plus ½ inch for two seam allowances and ⅛ inch to ¼ inch more to span the thickness of the quilt. The fatter the batting, the more you need to allow. Cut binding on straight grain. Press in half, wrong sides together and proceed.

A Final Note

This is not meant to be a complete "how to" quilt book. If you want more basic piecing, hand quilting and finishing information about Sampler quilts, ask for *The New Sampler Quilt* by Diana Leone, published by C&T Publishing. The book also includes great information about fabric selection and color study. For machine quilting information, *Learn to Machine Quilt in Just One Weekend* by Marti Michell, published by ASN Publishing, succinctly covers the basics.

Approximate Yardage Requirements				
Fabric, by Position in Quilt	**Throw**	**Twin**	**Queen/Full**	**King**
Theme fabric – alternate squares* final border and blocks	2–3¼ yards	3½–4⅞ yards	4–5⅝ yards	4¾–6⅝ yards
Setting and Corner Triangles	⅞ yard	1 yard	1¼ yards	1½ yards
Sashing and use in blocks	1 yard	1½ yards	2 yards	3 yards
Sashing Triangles and use in blocks	1 yard	1⅜ yards	1¾ yards	2¾ yards
Sashing Squares	¼ yard	¼ yard	⅜ yard	½ yard
Narrow Border and blocks	⅜ yard	⅝ yard	1 yard	1⅜ yards
Light background in blocks	¾ yard	1 to 1½ yards	1½ yards	2 yards
Three other fabrics for use in blocks	¼ to ½ yard each	⅜ to ⅝ yard each	½ to ¾ yard each	⅝ to ⅞ yard each
Binding (French fold)	½ yard	⅝ yard	⅞ yard	1⅛ yards
Backing	3½ yards	4¼ yards	6¼ yards	9 yards

*Low number means no special cutting–high number **should** allow special cutting including mitered corners on the borders, but each fabric is different. When doing special cuts, make sure you have allowed enough by positioning paper patterns over the design you want in the alternate block and carefully measuring the fabric for borders. The 8-inch outer border shown on these quilts may not be appropriate for the fabric you have chosen.

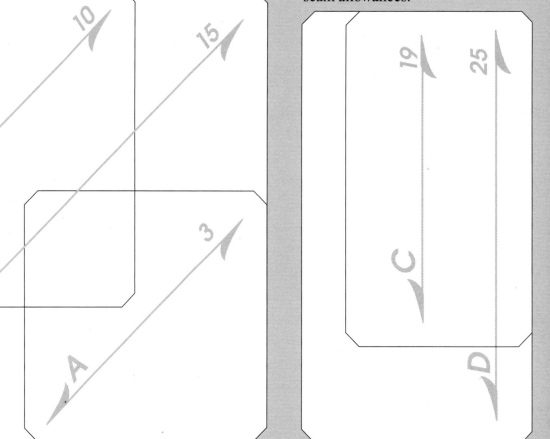

From

MARTI MICHELL ™

B

C

A

10

15

3

C

D

19

25

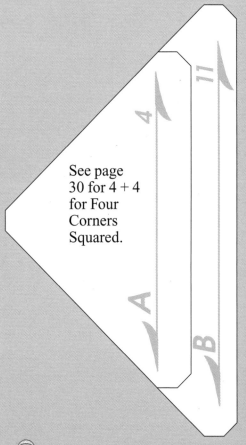

See page
30 for 4 + 4
for Four
Corners
Squared.

4

11

A

B

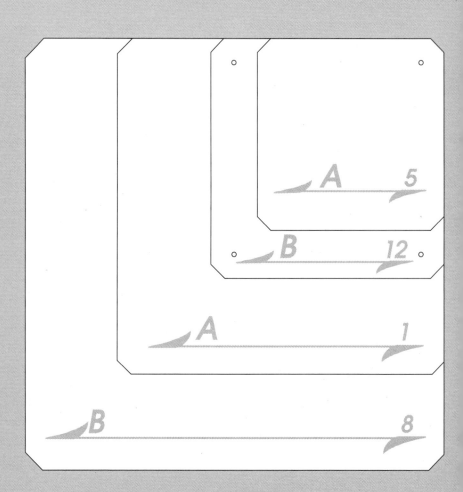

A

B

A

B

5

12

1

8

28

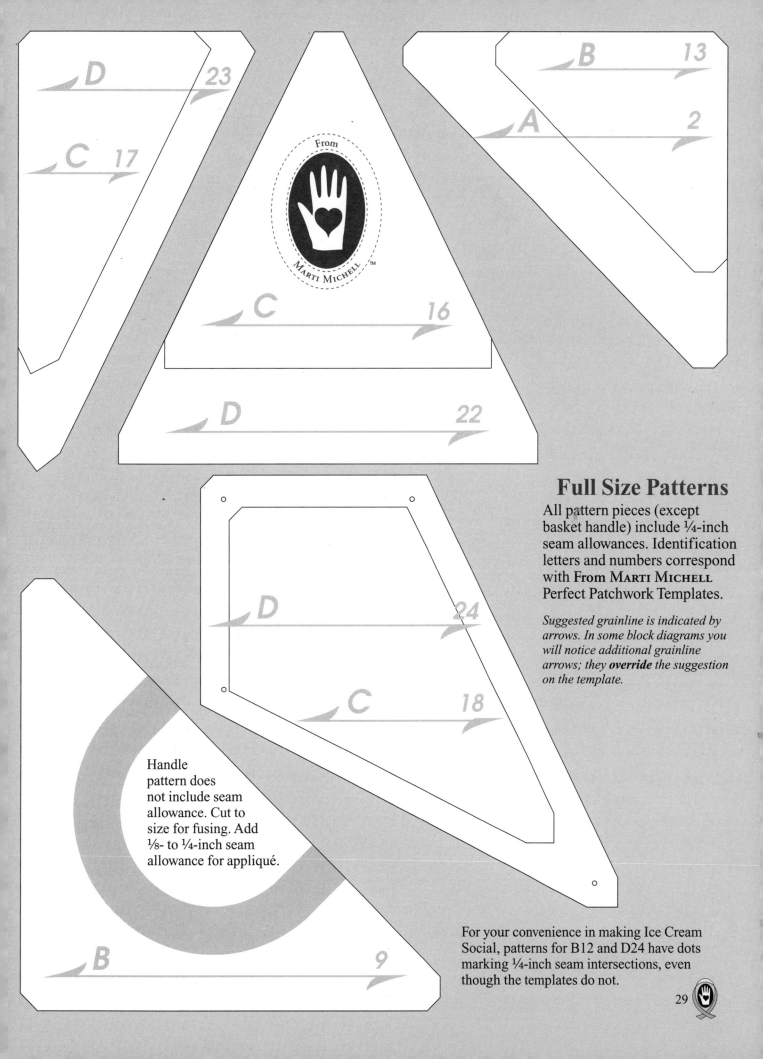

D 23

C 17

From
MARTI MICHELL ™

B 13

A 2

C 16

D 22

D 24

C 18

Full Size Patterns

All pattern pieces (except basket handle) include ¼-inch seam allowances. Identification letters and numbers correspond with **From MARTI MICHELL** Perfect Patchwork Templates.

*Suggested grainline is indicated by arrows. In some block diagrams you will notice additional grainline arrows; they **override** the suggestion on the template.*

Handle pattern does not include seam allowance. Cut to size for fusing. Add ⅛- to ¼-inch seam allowance for appliqué.

B 9

For your convenience in making Ice Cream Social, patterns for B12 and D24 have dots marking ¼-inch seam intersections, even though the templates do not.

Lillian's Flower Basket, *continued from page 22*

To make flowers, join four small squares into

Make 2 pieced triangles

For other 2 triangles, lay a #35 right side down on #32. Stitch ¼″ from edge of #35. Press in place.

Assemble like a diagonal half of an Eight-pointed Star, page 7. Assemble 2 halves to make the block.

match point

Full Size Patterns

All pattern pieces include ¼-inch seam allowances.

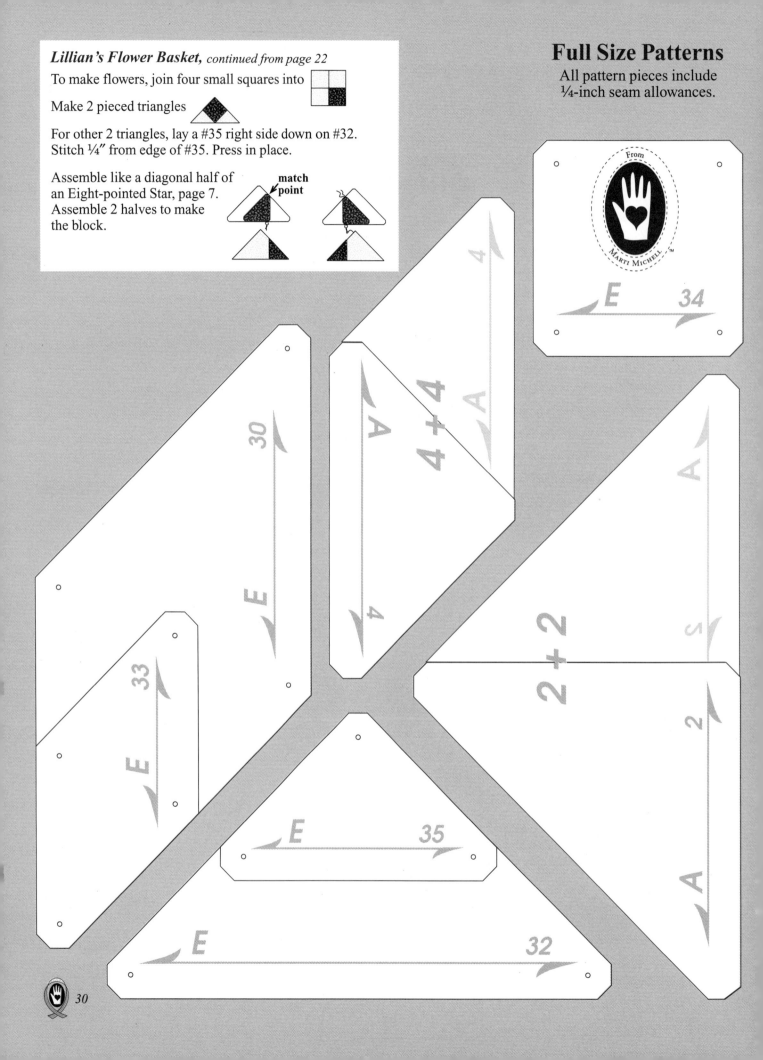

E   34

30

E

A
4 + 4
A

4

2 + 2

S

2

33

E

E   35

A

E   32

E

Copy and Color

All of the blocks in this book are collected on this page so that you can make several photocopies and use colored pencils to plan the blocks for your quilt. Don't forget to rotate the page so you can look at the blocks "on point" as you color. See page 32 for the page numbers of each block.

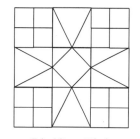

54-40 or Fight

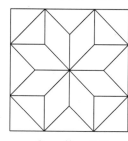

Carolina Lily

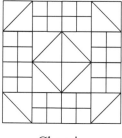

Cheerio

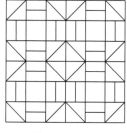

Churn Dash

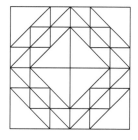

Corn 'n' Beans

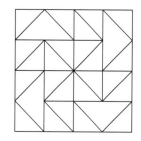

Dutchman's Pinwheel

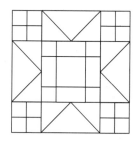

Northern Lights

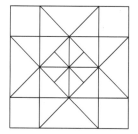

Pinwheel Variable Star

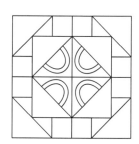

Postage Stamp Basket

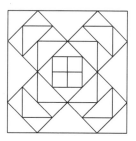

Rambler

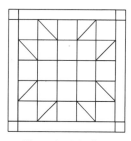

Sister's Choice

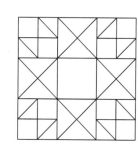

Sweet Sixteen

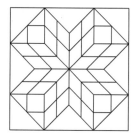

Bluegrass Needles

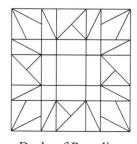

Buds of Paradise

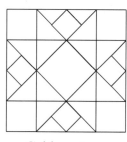

Cabbagetown

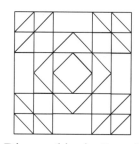

Diamond in the Rough

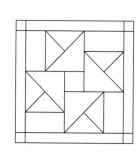

Double Starlight

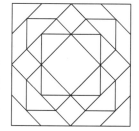

Four Corners Squared

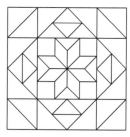

Grandmother's Favorite Star

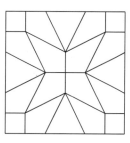

Ice Cream Social

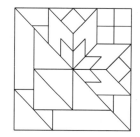

Lillian's Flower Basket

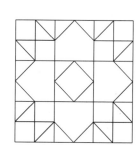

Weathervane Plus

Patchwork Block Directory

The 12 original blocks used in the 1997 *American Patchwork and Quilting* Sampler are listed here, followed by the 10 new blocks added for this book. Also listed are the template set or sets used and the number of pieces in each block to help you decide which blocks you want to make for your Sampler.

Block Name	Page No.	Template Set(s)	No. of Pieces
54-40 or Fight	12	B & D	33
Carolina Lily	12	E	20
Cheerio	13	A	48
Churn Dash	13	B	68
Corn 'n' Beans	14	B	48
Dutchman's Pinwheel	14	A	28
Northern Lights	15	A & C	37
Pinwheel Variable Star	15	A	28
Postage Stamp Basket	16	B	32
Rambler	16	A	40
Sister's Choice	17	B	41
Sweet Sixteen	17	B	41
New Perfect Patchwork Template Blocks			
*Bluegrass Needles**	18	E	52
Buds of Paradise	18	A & C	53
Cabbagetown	19	A & C	29
Diamond in the Rough	19	B & D	48
Double Starlight	20	B & D	25
Four Corners Squared	20	A & C	29
Grandmother's Favorite Star	21	A & E	48
Ice Cream Social	21	B & D	20 or 24
Lillian's Flower Basket	22	B & E	31 or 39
Weathervane Plus	22	B	41
Sashing		C	
Sashing Blocks		A	

Are Template Sets a Must?

"How many template sets do I really need?" you might ask. Pattern pieces are included for all of the shapes used in the blocks in this book, so you don't *need* any. However, most people who have used our template sets *want* all of them. Even though there are 17 different template sets at the time of printing this book, we have limited the Quilt for a Cure Sampler blocks to the first five sets. Sets A and B are the most frequently used. You really will love using Set C to make the sashing. With those three sets, you could template-cut all but seven blocks. However, if you want to use the three eight-pointed star blocks in your quilt, you'll want Set E; its cutting accuracy makes sewing easy. Set D adds the potential for some fun shapes in the 4-inch sub-unit.

The shapes are all so frequently used in patchwork that these blocks are just the beginning of the fun you can have making Sampler Quilts. See our *Encyclopedia of Patchwork Blocks, Volume 1*, for 69 blocks that can be made with Sets A or B, most in three sizes. *Volume 2* introduces 81 blocks made with Sets A and C or Sets B and D, and in *Volume 3*, there are 55 blocks that can be made with Set E.

*An aside to future researchers and those who play the quilt block name game; if the name is in italics, it is, to the best of our knowledge, a new name in this book. In most cases, it is a new design or a slightly altered familiar one.

The Quilt For a Cure Sampler Quilt

First Printing August 1999   Printed in the U.S.A.